This Book Belongs To:

WEBSITE

LOGIN

PASSWORD

NOTES

WEBSITE

LOGIN

PASSWORD

NOTES

WEBSITE

LOGIN

PASSWORD

NOTES

WEBSITE

LOGIN

PASSWORD

NOTES

WEBSITE

LOGIN

PASSWORD

NOTES

WEBSITE

LOGIN

PASSWORD

NOTES

WEBSITE

LOGIN

PASSWORD

NOTES

WEBSITE

LOGIN

PASSWORD

NOTES

WEBSITE

LOGIN

PASSWORD

NOTES

WEBSITE

LOGIN

PASSWORD

NOTES

WEBSITE

LOGIN

PASSWORD

NOTES

WEBSITE

LOGIN

PASSWORD

NOTES

WEBSITE

LOGIN

PASSWORD

NOTES

WEBSITE

LOGIN

PASSWORD

NOTES

WEBSITE

LOGIN

PASSWORD

NOTES

WEBSITE

LOGIN

PASSWORD

NOTES

WEBSITE

LOGIN

PASSWORD

NOTES

WEBSITE

LOGIN

PASSWORD

NOTES

WEBSITE

LOGIN

PASSWORD

NOTES

WEBSITE

LOGIN

PASSWORD

NOTES

WEBSITE

LOGIN

PASSWORD

NOTES

WEBSITE

LOGIN

PASSWORD

NOTES

WEBSITE

LOGIN

PASSWORD

NOTES

WEBSITE

LOGIN

PASSWORD

NOTES

WEBSITE

LOGIN

PASSWORD

NOTES

WEBSITE

LOGIN

PASSWORD

NOTES

WEBSITE

LOGIN

PASSWORD

NOTES

WEBSITE

LOGIN

PASSWORD

NOTES

WEBSITE

LOGIN

PASSWORD

NOTES

WEBSITE

LOGIN

PASSWORD

NOTES

WEBSITE

LOGIN

PASSWORD

NOTES

WEBSITE

LOGIN

PASSWORD

NOTES

WEBSITE

LOGIN

PASSWORD

NOTES

WEBSITE

LOGIN

PASSWORD

NOTES

WEBSITE

LOGIN

PASSWORD

NOTES

WEBSITE

LOGIN

PASSWORD

NOTES

WEBSITE

LOGIN

PASSWORD

NOTES

WEBSITE

LOGIN

PASSWORD

NOTES

WEBSITE

LOGIN

PASSWORD

NOTES

WEBSITE

LOGIN

PASSWORD

NOTES

WEBSITE

LOGIN

PASSWORD

NOTES

WEBSITE

LOGIN

PASSWORD

NOTES

WEBSITE

LOGIN

PASSWORD

NOTES

WEBSITE

LOGIN

PASSWORD

NOTES

WEBSITE

LOGIN

PASSWORD

NOTES

WEBSITE

LOGIN

PASSWORD

NOTES

WEBSITE

LOGIN

PASSWORD

NOTES

WEBSITE

LOGIN

PASSWORD

NOTES

WEBSITE

LOGIN

PASSWORD

NOTES

WEBSITE

LOGIN

PASSWORD

NOTES

WEBSITE

LOGIN

PASSWORD

NOTES

WEBSITE

LOGIN

PASSWORD

NOTES

WEBSITE

LOGIN

PASSWORD

NOTES

WEBSITE

LOGIN

PASSWORD

NOTES

WEBSITE

LOGIN

PASSWORD

NOTES

WEBSITE

LOGIN

PASSWORD

NOTES

WEBSITE

LOGIN

PASSWORD

NOTES

WEBSITE

LOGIN

PASSWORD

NOTES

WEBSITE

LOGIN

PASSWORD

NOTES

WEBSITE

LOGIN

PASSWORD

NOTES

WEBSITE

LOGIN

PASSWORD

NOTES

WEBSITE

LOGIN

PASSWORD

NOTES

WEBSITE

LOGIN

PASSWORD

NOTES

WEBSITE

LOGIN

PASSWORD

NOTES

WEBSITE

LOGIN

PASSWORD

NOTES

WEBSITE

LOGIN

PASSWORD

NOTES

WEBSITE

LOGIN

PASSWORD

NOTES

WEBSITE

LOGIN

PASSWORD

NOTES

WEBSITE

LOGIN

PASSWORD

NOTES

WEBSITE

LOGIN

PASSWORD

NOTES

WEBSITE

LOGIN

PASSWORD

NOTES

WEBSITE

LOGIN

PASSWORD

NOTES

WEBSITE

LOGIN

PASSWORD

NOTES

WEBSITE

LOGIN

PASSWORD

NOTES

WEBSITE

LOGIN

PASSWORD

NOTES

WEBSITE

LOGIN

PASSWORD

NOTES

WEBSITE

LOGIN

PASSWORD

NOTES

WEBSITE

LOGIN

PASSWORD

NOTES

WEBSITE

LOGIN

PASSWORD

NOTES

WEBSITE

LOGIN

PASSWORD

NOTES

WEBSITE

LOGIN

PASSWORD

NOTES

WEBSITE

LOGIN

PASSWORD

NOTES

WEBSITE

LOGIN

PASSWORD

NOTES

WEBSITE

LOGIN

PASSWORD

NOTES

WEBSITE

LOGIN

PASSWORD

NOTES

WEBSITE

LOGIN

PASSWORD

NOTES

WEBSITE

LOGIN

PASSWORD

NOTES

WEBSITE

LOGIN

PASSWORD

NOTES

WEBSITE

LOGIN

PASSWORD

NOTES

WEBSITE

LOGIN

PASSWORD

NOTES

WEBSITE

LOGIN

PASSWORD

NOTES

WEBSITE

LOGIN

PASSWORD

NOTES

WEBSITE

LOGIN

PASSWORD

NOTES

WEBSITE

LOGIN

PASSWORD

NOTES

WEBSITE

LOGIN

PASSWORD

NOTES

WEBSITE

LOGIN

PASSWORD

NOTES

WEBSITE

LOGIN

PASSWORD

NOTES

WEBSITE

LOGIN

PASSWORD

NOTES

WEBSITE

LOGIN

PASSWORD

NOTES

WEBSITE

LOGIN

PASSWORD

NOTES

WEBSITE

LOGIN

PASSWORD

NOTES

WEBSITE

LOGIN

PASSWORD

NOTES

WEBSITE

LOGIN

PASSWORD

NOTES

WEBSITE

LOGIN

PASSWORD

NOTES

WEBSITE

LOGIN

PASSWORD

NOTES

WEBSITE

LOGIN

PASSWORD

NOTES

WEBSITE

LOGIN

PASSWORD

NOTES

WEBSITE

LOGIN

PASSWORD

NOTES

WEBSITE

LOGIN

PASSWORD

NOTES

WEBSITE

LOGIN

PASSWORD

NOTES

WEBSITE

LOGIN

PASSWORD

NOTES

WEBSITE

LOGIN

PASSWORD

NOTES

WEBSITE

LOGIN

PASSWORD

NOTES

WEBSITE

LOGIN

PASSWORD

NOTES

WEBSITE

LOGIN

PASSWORD

NOTES

WEBSITE

LOGIN

PASSWORD

NOTES

WEBSITE

LOGIN

PASSWORD

NOTES

WEBSITE

LOGIN

PASSWORD

NOTES

WEBSITE

LOGIN

PASSWORD

NOTES

WEBSITE

LOGIN

PASSWORD

NOTES

WEBSITE

LOGIN

PASSWORD

NOTES

WEBSITE

LOGIN

PASSWORD

NOTES

WEBSITE

LOGIN

PASSWORD

NOTES

WEBSITE

LOGIN

PASSWORD

NOTES

WEBSITE

LOGIN

PASSWORD

NOTES

WEBSITE

LOGIN

PASSWORD

NOTES

WEBSITE

LOGIN

PASSWORD

NOTES

WEBSITE

LOGIN

PASSWORD

NOTES

WEBSITE

LOGIN

PASSWORD

NOTES

WEBSITE

LOGIN

PASSWORD

NOTES

WEBSITE

LOGIN

PASSWORD

NOTES

WEBSITE

LOGIN

PASSWORD

NOTES

WEBSITE

LOGIN

PASSWORD

NOTES

WEBSITE

LOGIN

PASSWORD

NOTES

WEBSITE

LOGIN

PASSWORD

NOTES

WEBSITE

LOGIN

PASSWORD

NOTES

WEBSITE

LOGIN

PASSWORD

NOTES

WEBSITE

LOGIN

PASSWORD

NOTES

WEBSITE

LOGIN

PASSWORD

NOTES

WEBSITE

LOGIN

PASSWORD

NOTES

WEBSITE

LOGIN

PASSWORD

NOTES

WEBSITE

LOGIN

PASSWORD

NOTES

WEBSITE

LOGIN

PASSWORD

NOTES

WEBSITE

LOGIN

PASSWORD

NOTES

WEBSITE

LOGIN

PASSWORD

NOTES

WEBSITE

LOGIN

PASSWORD

NOTES

WEBSITE

LOGIN

PASSWORD

NOTES

WEBSITE

LOGIN

PASSWORD

NOTES

WEBSITE

LOGIN

PASSWORD

NOTES

WEBSITE

LOGIN

PASSWORD

NOTES

WEBSITE

LOGIN

PASSWORD

NOTES

WEBSITE

LOGIN

PASSWORD

NOTES

WEBSITE

LOGIN

PASSWORD

NOTES

WEBSITE

LOGIN

PASSWORD

NOTES

WEBSITE

LOGIN

PASSWORD

NOTES

WEBSITE

LOGIN

PASSWORD

NOTES

WEBSITE

LOGIN

PASSWORD

NOTES

WEBSITE

LOGIN

PASSWORD

NOTES

WEBSITE

LOGIN

PASSWORD

NOTES

WEBSITE

LOGIN

PASSWORD

NOTES

WEBSITE

LOGIN

PASSWORD

NOTES

WEBSITE

LOGIN

PASSWORD

NOTES

WEBSITE

LOGIN

PASSWORD

NOTES

WEBSITE

LOGIN

PASSWORD

NOTES

WEBSITE

LOGIN

PASSWORD

NOTES

WEBSITE

LOGIN

PASSWORD

NOTES

WEBSITE

LOGIN

PASSWORD

NOTES

WEBSITE

LOGIN

PASSWORD

NOTES

WEBSITE

LOGIN

PASSWORD

NOTES

WEBSITE

LOGIN

PASSWORD

NOTES

WEBSITE

LOGIN

PASSWORD

NOTES

WEBSITE

LOGIN

PASSWORD

NOTES

WEBSITE

LOGIN

PASSWORD

NOTES

WEBSITE

LOGIN

PASSWORD

NOTES

WEBSITE

LOGIN

PASSWORD

NOTES

WEBSITE

LOGIN

PASSWORD

NOTES

WEBSITE

LOGIN

PASSWORD

NOTES

WEBSITE

LOGIN

PASSWORD

NOTES

WEBSITE

LOGIN

PASSWORD

NOTES

WEBSITE

LOGIN

PASSWORD

NOTES

WEBSITE

LOGIN

PASSWORD

NOTES

WEBSITE

LOGIN

PASSWORD

NOTES

WEBSITE

LOGIN

PASSWORD

NOTES

WEBSITE

LOGIN

PASSWORD

NOTES

WEBSITE

LOGIN

PASSWORD

NOTES

WEBSITE

LOGIN

PASSWORD

NOTES

WEBSITE

LOGIN

PASSWORD

NOTES

WEBSITE

LOGIN

PASSWORD

NOTES

WEBSITE

LOGIN

PASSWORD

NOTES

WEBSITE

LOGIN

PASSWORD

NOTES

WEBSITE

LOGIN

PASSWORD

NOTES

WEBSITE

LOGIN

PASSWORD

NOTES

WEBSITE

LOGIN

PASSWORD

NOTES

WEBSITE

LOGIN

PASSWORD

NOTES

WEBSITE

LOGIN

PASSWORD

NOTES

WEBSITE

LOGIN

PASSWORD

NOTES

WEBSITE

LOGIN

PASSWORD

NOTES

WEBSITE

LOGIN

PASSWORD

NOTES

WEBSITE

LOGIN

PASSWORD

NOTES

WEBSITE

LOGIN

PASSWORD

NOTES

WEBSITE

LOGIN

PASSWORD

NOTES

WEBSITE

LOGIN

PASSWORD

NOTES

WEBSITE

LOGIN

PASSWORD

NOTES

WEBSITE

LOGIN

PASSWORD

NOTES

WEBSITE

LOGIN

PASSWORD

NOTES

WEBSITE

LOGIN

PASSWORD

NOTES

WEBSITE

LOGIN

PASSWORD

NOTES

WEBSITE

LOGIN

PASSWORD

NOTES

WEBSITE

LOGIN

PASSWORD

NOTES

WEBSITE

LOGIN

PASSWORD

NOTES

WEBSITE

LOGIN

PASSWORD

NOTES

WEBSITE

LOGIN

PASSWORD

NOTES

WEBSITE

LOGIN

PASSWORD

NOTES

WEBSITE

LOGIN

PASSWORD

NOTES

WEBSITE

LOGIN

PASSWORD

NOTES

WEBSITE

LOGIN

PASSWORD

NOTES

WEBSITE

LOGIN

PASSWORD

NOTES

WEBSITE

LOGIN

PASSWORD

NOTES

WEBSITE

LOGIN

PASSWORD

NOTES

WEBSITE

LOGIN

PASSWORD

NOTES

WEBSITE

LOGIN

PASSWORD

NOTES

WEBSITE

LOGIN

PASSWORD

NOTES

WEBSITE

LOGIN

PASSWORD

NOTES

WEBSITE

LOGIN

PASSWORD

NOTES

WEBSITE

LOGIN

PASSWORD

NOTES

WEBSITE

LOGIN

PASSWORD

NOTES

WEBSITE

LOGIN

PASSWORD

NOTES

WEBSITE

LOGIN

PASSWORD

NOTES

WEBSITE

LOGIN

PASSWORD

NOTES

WEBSITE

LOGIN

PASSWORD

NOTES

WEBSITE

LOGIN

PASSWORD

NOTES

WEBSITE

LOGIN

PASSWORD

NOTES

WEBSITE

LOGIN

PASSWORD

NOTES

WEBSITE

LOGIN

PASSWORD

NOTES

WEBSITE

LOGIN

PASSWORD

NOTES

WEBSITE

LOGIN

PASSWORD

NOTES

WEBSITE

LOGIN

PASSWORD

NOTES

WEBSITE

LOGIN

PASSWORD

NOTES

WEBSITE

LOGIN

PASSWORD

NOTES

WEBSITE

LOGIN

PASSWORD

NOTES

WEBSITE

LOGIN

PASSWORD

NOTES

WEBSITE

LOGIN

PASSWORD

NOTES

WEBSITE

LOGIN

PASSWORD

NOTES

WEBSITE

LOGIN

PASSWORD

NOTES

WEBSITE

LOGIN

PASSWORD

NOTES

WEBSITE

LOGIN

PASSWORD

NOTES

WEBSITE

LOGIN

PASSWORD

NOTES

WEBSITE

LOGIN

PASSWORD

NOTES

WEBSITE

LOGIN

PASSWORD

NOTES

WEBSITE

LOGIN

PASSWORD

NOTES

WEBSITE

LOGIN

PASSWORD

NOTES

WEBSITE

LOGIN

PASSWORD

NOTES

WEBSITE

LOGIN

PASSWORD

NOTES

WEBSITE

LOGIN

PASSWORD

NOTES

WEBSITE

LOGIN

PASSWORD

NOTES

WEBSITE

LOGIN

PASSWORD

NOTES

WEBSITE

LOGIN

PASSWORD

NOTES

WEBSITE

LOGIN

PASSWORD

NOTES

WEBSITE

LOGIN

PASSWORD

NOTES

WEBSITE

LOGIN

PASSWORD

NOTES

WEBSITE

LOGIN

PASSWORD

NOTES

WEBSITE

LOGIN

PASSWORD

NOTES

WEBSITE

LOGIN

PASSWORD

NOTES

WEBSITE

LOGIN

PASSWORD

NOTES

WEBSITE

LOGIN

PASSWORD

NOTES

WEBSITE

LOGIN

PASSWORD

NOTES

WEBSITE

LOGIN

PASSWORD

NOTES

WEBSITE

LOGIN

PASSWORD

NOTES

WEBSITE

LOGIN

PASSWORD

NOTES

WEBSITE

LOGIN

PASSWORD

NOTES

WEBSITE

LOGIN

PASSWORD

NOTES

WEBSITE

LOGIN

PASSWORD

NOTES

WEBSITE

LOGIN

PASSWORD

NOTES

WEBSITE

LOGIN

PASSWORD

NOTES

WEBSITE

LOGIN

PASSWORD

NOTES

WEBSITE

LOGIN

PASSWORD

NOTES

WEBSITE

LOGIN

PASSWORD

NOTES

WEBSITE

LOGIN

PASSWORD

NOTES

WEBSITE

LOGIN

PASSWORD

NOTES

WEBSITE

LOGIN

PASSWORD

NOTES

WEBSITE

LOGIN

PASSWORD

NOTES

WEBSITE

LOGIN

PASSWORD

NOTES

WEBSITE

LOGIN

PASSWORD

NOTES

WEBSITE

LOGIN

PASSWORD

NOTES

WEBSITE

LOGIN

PASSWORD

NOTES

WEBSITE

LOGIN

PASSWORD

NOTES

WEBSITE

LOGIN

PASSWORD

NOTES

WEBSITE

LOGIN

PASSWORD

NOTES

WEBSITE

LOGIN

PASSWORD

NOTES

WEBSITE

LOGIN

PASSWORD

NOTES

WEBSITE

LOGIN

PASSWORD

NOTES

WEBSITE

LOGIN

PASSWORD

NOTES

WEBSITE

LOGIN

PASSWORD

NOTES

WEBSITE

LOGIN

PASSWORD

NOTES

WEBSITE

LOGIN

PASSWORD

NOTES

WEBSITE

LOGIN

PASSWORD

NOTES

WEBSITE

LOGIN

PASSWORD

NOTES

WEBSITE

LOGIN

PASSWORD

NOTES

WEBSITE

LOGIN

PASSWORD

NOTES

WEBSITE

LOGIN

PASSWORD

NOTES

WEBSITE

LOGIN

PASSWORD

NOTES

WEBSITE

LOGIN

PASSWORD

NOTES

WEBSITE

LOGIN

PASSWORD

NOTES

WEBSITE

LOGIN

PASSWORD

NOTES

WEBSITE

LOGIN

PASSWORD

NOTES

WEBSITE

LOGIN

PASSWORD

NOTES

WEBSITE

LOGIN

PASSWORD

NOTES

WEBSITE

LOGIN

PASSWORD

NOTES

WEBSITE

LOGIN

PASSWORD

NOTES

WEBSITE

LOGIN

PASSWORD

NOTES

WEBSITE

LOGIN

PASSWORD

NOTES

WEBSITE

LOGIN

PASSWORD

NOTES

WEBSITE

LOGIN

PASSWORD

NOTES

WEBSITE

LOGIN

PASSWORD

NOTES

WEBSITE

LOGIN

PASSWORD

NOTES

WEBSITE

LOGIN

PASSWORD

NOTES

WEBSITE

LOGIN

PASSWORD

NOTES

WEBSITE

LOGIN

PASSWORD

NOTES

WEBSITE

LOGIN

PASSWORD

NOTES

WEBSITE

LOGIN

PASSWORD

NOTES

WEBSITE

LOGIN

PASSWORD

NOTES

WEBSITE

LOGIN

PASSWORD

NOTES

WEBSITE

LOGIN

PASSWORD

NOTES

WEBSITE

LOGIN

PASSWORD

NOTES

WEBSITE

LOGIN

PASSWORD

NOTES

WEBSITE

LOGIN

PASSWORD

NOTES

WEBSITE

LOGIN

PASSWORD

NOTES

WEBSITE

LOGIN

PASSWORD

NOTES

WEBSITE

LOGIN

PASSWORD

NOTES

WEBSITE

LOGIN

PASSWORD

NOTES

WEBSITE

LOGIN

PASSWORD

NOTES

WEBSITE

LOGIN

PASSWORD

NOTES

WEBSITE

LOGIN

PASSWORD

NOTES

WEBSITE

LOGIN

PASSWORD

NOTES

WEBSITE

LOGIN

PASSWORD

NOTES

WEBSITE

LOGIN

PASSWORD

NOTES

WEBSITE

LOGIN

PASSWORD

NOTES

WEBSITE

LOGIN

PASSWORD

NOTES

WEBSITE

LOGIN

PASSWORD

NOTES

WEBSITE

LOGIN

PASSWORD

NOTES

WEBSITE

LOGIN

PASSWORD

NOTES

WEBSITE

LOGIN

PASSWORD

NOTES

WEBSITE

LOGIN

PASSWORD

NOTES

WEBSITE

LOGIN

PASSWORD

NOTES

WEBSITE

LOGIN

PASSWORD

NOTES

WEBSITE

LOGIN

PASSWORD

NOTES

WEBSITE

LOGIN

PASSWORD

NOTES

WEBSITE

LOGIN

PASSWORD

NOTES

WEBSITE

LOGIN

PASSWORD

NOTES

WEBSITE

LOGIN

PASSWORD

NOTES

WEBSITE

LOGIN

PASSWORD

NOTES

WEBSITE

LOGIN

PASSWORD

NOTES

WEBSITE

LOGIN

PASSWORD

NOTES

WEBSITE

LOGIN

PASSWORD

NOTES

WEBSITE

LOGIN

PASSWORD

NOTES

WEBSITE

LOGIN

PASSWORD

NOTES

WEBSITE

LOGIN

PASSWORD

NOTES

WEBSITE

LOGIN

PASSWORD

NOTES

WEBSITE

LOGIN

PASSWORD

NOTES

WEBSITE

LOGIN

PASSWORD

NOTES

WEBSITE

LOGIN

PASSWORD

NOTES

WEBSITE

LOGIN

PASSWORD

NOTES

WEBSITE

LOGIN

PASSWORD

NOTES

WEBSITE

LOGIN

PASSWORD

NOTES

WEBSITE

LOGIN

PASSWORD

NOTES

WEBSITE

LOGIN

PASSWORD

NOTES

WEBSITE

LOGIN

PASSWORD

NOTES

WEBSITE

LOGIN

PASSWORD

NOTES

WEBSITE

LOGIN

PASSWORD

NOTES

WEBSITE

LOGIN

PASSWORD

NOTES

WEBSITE

LOGIN

PASSWORD

NOTES

WEBSITE

LOGIN

PASSWORD

NOTES

WEBSITE

LOGIN

PASSWORD

NOTES

WEBSITE

LOGIN

PASSWORD

NOTES

WEBSITE

LOGIN

PASSWORD

NOTES

WEBSITE

LOGIN

PASSWORD

NOTES

WEBSITE

LOGIN

PASSWORD

NOTES

WEBSITE

LOGIN

PASSWORD

NOTES

WEBSITE

LOGIN

PASSWORD

NOTES

WEBSITE

LOGIN

PASSWORD

NOTES

WEBSITE

LOGIN

PASSWORD

NOTES

WEBSITE

LOGIN

PASSWORD

NOTES

WEBSITE

LOGIN

PASSWORD

NOTES

WEBSITE

LOGIN

PASSWORD

NOTES

WEBSITE

LOGIN

PASSWORD

NOTES

WEBSITE

LOGIN

PASSWORD

NOTES

WEBSITE

LOGIN

PASSWORD

NOTES

WEBSITE

LOGIN

PASSWORD

NOTES

WEBSITE

LOGIN

PASSWORD

NOTES

WEBSITE

LOGIN

PASSWORD

NOTES

WEBSITE

LOGIN

PASSWORD

NOTES

WEBSITE

LOGIN

PASSWORD

NOTES

WEBSITE

LOGIN

PASSWORD

NOTES

WEBSITE

LOGIN

PASSWORD

NOTES

WEBSITE

LOGIN

PASSWORD

NOTES

WEBSITE

LOGIN

PASSWORD

NOTES

WEBSITE

LOGIN

PASSWORD

NOTES

WEBSITE

LOGIN

PASSWORD

NOTES

WEBSITE

LOGIN

PASSWORD

NOTES

WEBSITE

LOGIN

PASSWORD

NOTES

WEBSITE

LOGIN

PASSWORD

NOTES

WEBSITE

LOGIN

PASSWORD

NOTES

WEBSITE

LOGIN

PASSWORD

NOTES

WEBSITE

LOGIN

PASSWORD

NOTES

WEBSITE

LOGIN

PASSWORD

NOTES

WEBSITE

LOGIN

PASSWORD

NOTES

WEBSITE

LOGIN

PASSWORD

NOTES

WEBSITE

LOGIN

PASSWORD

NOTES

WEBSITE

LOGIN

PASSWORD

NOTES

WEBSITE

LOGIN

PASSWORD

NOTES

WEBSITE

LOGIN

PASSWORD

NOTES

WEBSITE

LOGIN

PASSWORD

NOTES

WEBSITE

LOGIN

PASSWORD

NOTES

WEBSITE

LOGIN

PASSWORD

NOTES

WEBSITE

LOGIN

PASSWORD

NOTES

WEBSITE

LOGIN

PASSWORD

NOTES

WEBSITE

LOGIN

PASSWORD

NOTES

WEBSITE

LOGIN

PASSWORD

NOTES

WEBSITE

LOGIN

PASSWORD

NOTES

WEBSITE

LOGIN

PASSWORD

NOTES

WEBSITE

LOGIN

PASSWORD

NOTES

WEBSITE

LOGIN

PASSWORD

NOTES

WEBSITE

LOGIN

PASSWORD

NOTES

WEBSITE

LOGIN

PASSWORD

NOTES

WEBSITE

LOGIN

PASSWORD

NOTES

WEBSITE

LOGIN

PASSWORD

NOTES

WEBSITE

LOGIN

PASSWORD

NOTES

WEBSITE

LOGIN

PASSWORD

NOTES

WEBSITE

LOGIN

PASSWORD

NOTES

WEBSITE

LOGIN

PASSWORD

NOTES

WEBSITE

LOGIN

PASSWORD

NOTES

WEBSITE

LOGIN

PASSWORD

NOTES

WEBSITE

LOGIN

PASSWORD

NOTES

WEBSITE

LOGIN

PASSWORD

NOTES

WEBSITE

LOGIN

PASSWORD

NOTES

WEBSITE

LOGIN

PASSWORD

NOTES

WEBSITE

LOGIN

PASSWORD

NOTES

WEBSITE

LOGIN

PASSWORD

NOTES

WEBSITE

LOGIN

PASSWORD

NOTES

WEBSITE

LOGIN

PASSWORD

NOTES

WEBSITE

LOGIN

PASSWORD

NOTES

WEBSITE

LOGIN

PASSWORD

NOTES

WEBSITE

LOGIN

PASSWORD

NOTES

WEBSITE

LOGIN

PASSWORD

NOTES

WEBSITE

LOGIN

PASSWORD

NOTES

WEBSITE

LOGIN

PASSWORD

NOTES

WEBSITE

LOGIN

PASSWORD

NOTES

WEBSITE

LOGIN

PASSWORD

NOTES

WEBSITE

LOGIN

PASSWORD

NOTES

WEBSITE

LOGIN

PASSWORD

NOTES

WEBSITE

LOGIN

PASSWORD

NOTES

WEBSITE

LOGIN

PASSWORD

NOTES

WEBSITE

LOGIN

PASSWORD

NOTES

WEBSITE

LOGIN

PASSWORD

NOTES

WEBSITE

LOGIN

PASSWORD

NOTES

WEBSITE

LOGIN

PASSWORD

NOTES

WEBSITE

LOGIN

PASSWORD

NOTES

WEBSITE

LOGIN

PASSWORD

NOTES

WEBSITE

LOGIN

PASSWORD

NOTES

WEBSITE

LOGIN

PASSWORD

NOTES

WEBSITE

LOGIN

PASSWORD

NOTES

WEBSITE

LOGIN

PASSWORD

NOTES

WEBSITE

LOGIN

PASSWORD

NOTES

WEBSITE

LOGIN

PASSWORD

NOTES

WEBSITE

LOGIN

PASSWORD

NOTES

WEBSITE

LOGIN

PASSWORD

NOTES

WEBSITE

LOGIN

PASSWORD

NOTES

WEBSITE

LOGIN

PASSWORD

NOTES

WEBSITE

LOGIN

PASSWORD

NOTES

WEBSITE

LOGIN

PASSWORD

NOTES

WEBSITE

LOGIN

PASSWORD

NOTES

WEBSITE

LOGIN

PASSWORD

NOTES

WEBSITE

LOGIN

PASSWORD

NOTES

WEBSITE

LOGIN

PASSWORD

NOTES

WEBSITE

LOGIN

PASSWORD

NOTES

WEBSITE

LOGIN

PASSWORD

NOTES

WEBSITE

LOGIN

PASSWORD

NOTES

WEBSITE

LOGIN

PASSWORD

NOTES

WEBSITE

LOGIN

PASSWORD

NOTES

WEBSITE

LOGIN

PASSWORD

NOTES